A Leaf's Life

Matthew Clemente

AuthorHouse™
1663 Liberty Drive
Bloomington, IN 47403
www.authorhouse.com
Phone: 1 (800) 839-8640

Published by AuthorHouse   06/26/2018

ISBN: 978-1-5462-4836-1 (sc)
ISBN: 978-1-5462-4837-8 (e)

authorHOUSE®

A Leaf's Life

We leaves don't live very long. We're born in the spring while the birds sing their song.

We start out as buds that grow on a stem. We receive water from our trees and we return food to them.

Speaking of which, we too can be a food fest by insects such as slugs and snails, who are also known as pests.

And just like a snow flake, no two leaves are alike. We have veins that run through us and we're truly unique.

As autumn comes, we start to change from our vibrant green color to red, brown, and orange.

This means that our work is almost done. Next, we float to the ground, waving goodbye to the sun.

That's the end of our
cycle when it comes to
our work, but as for play
we have one fun perk.

Cause it's true we make lots of people smile. When you rake us all up, you can jump in our pile.

Although the trees are bare, don't feel grief, 'cause come next spring they'll turn over a new leaf!

Printed in the United States
By Bookmasters